A LifeGuide® *Bible Study*

CHRISTIAN VIRTUES

9 studies
for individuals or groups
Cindy Bunch

With Notes for Leaders

InterVarsity Press
Downers Grove, Illinois

InterVarsity Press
P.O. Box 1400, Downers Grove, IL 60515
World Wide Web: www.ivpress.com
E-mail: mail@ivpress.com

InterVarsity Press® is the book-publishing division of InterVarsity Christian Fellowship®, a student movement active on campus at hundreds of universities, colleges and schools of nursing in the United States of America, and a member movement of the International Fellowship of Evangelical Students. For information about local and regional activities, write Public Relations Dept., InterVarsity Christian Fellowship, 6400 Schroeder Rd., P.O. Box 7895, Madison, WI 53707-7895.

Cover image: Daryl Benson/Masterfile

ISBN 0-8308-3079-0

Printed in the United States of America ∞

P	17	16	15	14	13	12	11	10	9	8	7	6	5	4
Y	16	15	14	13	12	11	10	09	08	07	06	05		

Contents

Getting the Most Out of
Christian Virtues

Going to Sunday school was an integral part of my grandfather's life. From the time Leland Bunch Sr. was five years old until he died just seven months short of the seventy-fifth anniversary of that commitment, he never missed Sunday school.

If Leland was traveling, then he went to the nearest church—Baptist, if possible. For instance, one Sunday during World War II, while flying on military duty with the Red Cross from one post to another, he convinced the helicopter pilot to land the plane so that he could go to Sunday school. The pilot, who hadn't been to church in years, was convinced to go with him. In later life golfing was Leland's passion. When he was participating in a weekend golf tournament at the local club, my grandmother would pick him up at the fourth hole, which was next to the highway. She would give him a bow tie, take him to Sunday school and then bring him back to catch up with the rest of the foursome. He would just take an average score for the holes he missed, perhaps surprising a few golfing partners who felt the tournament was more important than a weekly opportunity like Sunday school.

When Leland was hospitalized a few times, his class came to him! Such was the commitment of this Christian community to their time of Bible learning together. Members of this class continue to meet together to this day.

Virtues are contagious. People were touched by Leland's commitment throughout his life, and the impact continues since his death. Knowing that their father's last wish in life was to make it to his seventy-fifth Sunday school anniversary, Uncle David and my father, Fred, finished out those last seven months of Leland's Sunday school attendance record. Uncle David went to Leland's long-standing class at Fifth Avenue Baptist Church. Fred, living in a different city, attended class and began teaching as well. The discipline of following in Leland Bunch Sr.'s footsteps has renewed their commitment to studying the Bible.

Some might say that my grandfather was a man typical of his era—persevering, steadily following the same truths of his faith decade after decade—a man who valued qualities that mean little to people today. Even the idea of keeping track of Sunday school attendance may seem quaint, eccentric or legalistic. But he was a man of virtue; he lived consistently with his beliefs.

What About Virtue?
Complaints about the state of virtue in our culture are common. I've heard more than one person say something like "Kids aren't being taught basic manners by their parents anymore." And a teacher recently commented that essential moral values once taught at home are now being left to the public schools to instill.

Though many are pessimistic about the state of culture, the success of William Bennett's *Book of Virtues* in the nineties also suggests there's a hunger for stories of virtue. For most of us, virtue is attractive. When we find a person we can trust, then that's a person we want to stick with.

The strongest reason to study virtue predates William Bennett's book and my grandfather. Long before the bestseller lists began, God set some standards for us, and one of the fruits of knowing him is that he grows us into people of virtue.

What are the virtues God values? Consider, for example, the

fruits of the Spirit, the description of love in Romans 12:9-16 and the list in 2 Peter 1:5-6. From these and other biblical passages I have selected a sampling that can serve as groundwork for building a strong Christian character. Studies 1-3 begin with the inner virtues of faith, hope and love—the essential attitudes out of which all the others arise. Studies 4-9 deal with the actions or outworking of these attitudes: wisdom, justice, courage, moderation, integrity and perseverance.

These are big topics. We will spend our whole lives learning to understand and apply them. Yet I hope that each of these studies will leave you with one new insight about the virtue being discussed and an idea about how it can be enacted in your life.

May God bless your desire to become a person of virtue.

Suggestions for Individual Study

1. As you begin each study, pray that God will speak to you through his Word.

2. Read the introduction to the study and respond to the personal reflection question or exercise. This is designed to help you focus on God and on the theme of the study.

3. Each study deals with a particular passage—so that you can delve into the author's meaning in that context. Read and reread the passage to be studied. The questions are written using the language of the New International Version, so you may wish to use that version of the Bible. The New Revised Standard Version is also recommended.

4. This is an inductive Bible study, designed to help you discover for yourself what Scripture is saying. The study includes three types of questions. *Observation* questions ask about the basic facts: who, what, when, where and how. *Interpretation* questions delve into the meaning of the passage. *Application* questions help you discover the implications of the text for growing in Christ. These three keys unlock the treasures of Scripture.

Write your answers to the questions in the spaces provided or in a personal journal. Writing can bring clarity and deeper understanding of yourself and of God's Word.

5. It might be good to have a Bible dictionary handy. Use it to look up any unfamiliar words, names or places.

6. Use the prayer suggestion to guide you in thanking God for what you have learned and to pray about the applications that have come to mind.

7. You may want to go on to the suggestion under "Now or Later," or you may want to use that idea for your next study.

Suggestions for Members of a Group Study

1. Come to the study prepared. Follow the suggestions for individual study mentioned above. You will find that careful preparation will greatly enrich your time spent in group discussion.

2. Be willing to participate in the discussion. The leader of your group will not be lecturing. Instead, he or she will be encouraging the members of the group to discuss what they have learned. The leader will be asking the questions that are found in this guide.

3. Stick to the topic being discussed. Your answers should be based on the verses which are the focus of the discussion and not on outside authorities such as commentaries or speakers. These studies focus on a particular passage of Scripture. Only rarely should you refer to other portions of the Bible. This allows for everyone to participate in in-depth study on equal ground.

4. Be sensitive to the other members of the group. Listen attentively when they describe what they have learned. You may be surprised by their insights! Each question assumes a variety of answers. Many questions do not have "right" answers, particularly questions that aim at meaning or application. Instead the questions push us to explore the passage more thoroughly. When possible, link what you say to the comments of others. Also, be affirming whenever you can. This will encourage some of the more hesitant members of the group to participate.

5. Be careful not to dominate the discussion. We are sometimes so eager to express our thoughts that we leave too little opportunity for others to respond. By all means participate! But allow others to also.

6. Expect God to teach you through the passage being discussed and through the other members of the group. Pray that you will have an enjoyable and profitable time together, but also that as a result of the study you will find ways that you can take action individually and/or as a group.

7. Remember that anything said in the group is considered confidential and should not be discussed outside the group unless specific permission is given to do so.

8. If you are the group leader, you will find additional suggestions at the back of the guide.

1

Faith

Some of us approach faith through our brains. We work out the details through logic, reading and debate with others and finally assent to it when it makes sense. Others of us approach faith through our hearts. We need to experience a sense that God is present and real and find that presence through worship, music, the testimony of others and prayer. All of us need both qualities, but we tend to make one or the other primary.

GROUP DISCUSSION. Describe one of the key head or heart steps in your process of coming to faith.

PERSONAL REFLECTION. Is faith something you feel and experience or something you think about and try to understand? Explain.

Read Ephesians 1:11-23.

1. What do these verses reveal about the role of each of the three persons of the Trinity?

2. What thoughts and feelings do you have as you read of what God has done?

3. What does it mean to be chosen by God (v. 11; see also v. 4)?

4. How did the Ephesians respond to God (vv. 13-15)?

5. In verse 15 Paul draws a connection between the Ephesians' faith and their love. How does your faith help you to love others?

6. When have you seen "faith" (Christian or other) that led someone away from loving others?

7. What does Paul ask God to do for the Ephesians (vv. 17-19)?

Why would he single out these qualities?

8. How does knowledge of God help make faith real?

9. How does the experience of God help make faith real?

10. Focus on your weaker area. What steps might help you grow in either your head or your heart faith?

---

11. When are you likely to see faith as something you need to "work on" rather than trusting God to build faith in you?

How can the facts in this passage enable you to escape that trap?

Offer your praise to God for the gift of faith.

Now or Later
This week focus on deepening your understanding of what nurtures and upholds your faith and what challenges it.

2

Hope

Despite a life of loving God and experiencing God's protection and forgiveness, as an aging man looking toward a menacing future David wondered where God was. Would the God who had been there throughout his life continue to protect him from his enemies? Where could he find hope?

GROUP DISCUSSION. What causes you to question God's work in the world or in your own life?

PERSONAL REFLECTION. Speak whatever hard questions you have for God now.

Read Psalm 71.

1. In Hebrew this psalm has six stanzas following a five-four-five line pattern. What is the theme of each of the sections: verses 1-4, 5-8, 9-13, 14-18, 19-21, 22-24?

2. How does David's tone change from stanza to stanza?

3. Which section do you most strongly identify with? Why?

4. What words and images in verses 1-4 reveal David's pleading tone?

5. How has God given David hope throughout his life (vv. 5-8)?

6. What is at the root of David's sense of hopelessness (vv. 9-13, 18)?

7. When have you had similar feelings of hopelessness?

8. What might be at the root of your hopelessness?

9. What are the sources of David's praise in verses 14-24?

---

10. Praising God brings a shift in David's mood by the end of these verses. How can praising God bring hope to our lives?

Even though circumstances may trigger hopelessness, praise God for the things he has done which give you confidence.

Now or Later
Make an ongoing list of things that bring hope to your life.

3

Love

1 John 3:11-20

Remember the TV show *Love, American Style* from the seventies? I recall watching reruns of it on the sly as a kid (it was forbidden viewing in my house). In the context of that show "sex" would be the essential definition of *love*.

How about *Love Boat,* an eighties show? Each week it would end with neatly matched pairs—many who had just met in a shipboard romance. In that show love was often connected to initial attraction. Love was something that could happen in the course of a week. "Infatuation" would be another way to describe this emotion.

In the nineties we didn't have "love," we had *Friends.* Friends who slept together and dated and broke up—and had children together. The show told us that love comes and goes but friendship endures.

And now we have *Sex in the City.* The relationships come and go at the speed of the designer fashions the characters wear.

GROUP DISCUSSION. What types of love tend to be overlooked by the media?

PERSONAL REFLECTION. In what ways are you vulnerable to the

media's depictions of love?

For a true picture of love in all its facets, the only reliable source is Scripture. *Read 1 John 3:11-20.*

1. What is striking to you about this description of love?

2. What actions and attitudes are contrary to love?

3. What actions and attitudes are signs of love?

4. How does the example of Cain (v. 12) illustrate the effects of jealousy on love between family members?

5. Why would the world hate Christians who show love?

---

6. How is *love* defined in verse 16?

---

7. How have you seen Christians either literally or metaphorically "lay down their lives" for one another?

---

8. Why is loving with actions more important than loving with words (vv. 17-18)?

9. How do our acts of love help strengthen our relationship with God (vv. 19-20)?

10. Whose actions have helped you understand the love of Christ?

11. How can you show someone love through your actions this week?

Ask God to help you grow in your knowledge of him so that love will flow out from you.

Now or Later

Continue your study of love by watching people around you. What can you learn about expressing godly love?

4

Wisdom

1 Corinthians 1:18-31

A college student drops his plans to pursue a law degree and goes overseas as a missionary.

A young woman refuses to work the sixteen-hour days that are required to move up the corporate ladder so that she can work with the youth group in her church.

A businessman in his forties leaves his career and moves his family and children to another state to begin seminary.

A retired couple puts their lifetime savings into a Christian bookstore to serve their community.

Each of these decisions might be regarded as wise or foolish depending on who you ask. And it is not just non-Christians who disagree about whether these are good decisions—Christians would have different views about them as well.

GROUP DISCUSSION. When has a person you regarded as wise taken a surprising (and perhaps foolish) risk?

PERSONAL REFLECTION. What risk (for God) do you regret not taking?

This passage is all about what constitutes wisdom and foolishness. *Read 1 Corinthians 1:18-31.*

1. In what ways are wisdom and foolishness contrasted in this passage?

2. How do you react to the way in which foolishness is described here?

3. Why is the cross wisdom to some but foolishness to others (vv. 18, 23-24)?

4. How would you define *foolishness* from this text?

5. How does God's view of wisdom contrast with the world's view (vv. 19-21)?

6. In what ways do many "wise" people today—scholars, philosophers, scientists—try to get along without God?

7. What aspect of the world's so-called wisdom has swayed you?

8. Notice the contrast between wisdom and strength (vv. 26-29). What value does social standing have in God's eyes?

9. What does Christ offer us (vv. 24, 30)?

What difference do these gifts make in our lives?

10. What does it mean to boast in the Lord (v. 31)?

11. From this passage how would you define *wisdom?*

12. How can you go about pursuing the wisdom of God?

Pray that God will make you wise in his ways.

Now or Later

Think of the Christian people you know. Who is a model of wisdom and why?

5

Justice

I once had an opportunity to visit a small urban courtroom where my cousin, a prosecutor, was at work. The hearing involved a man who had been convicted of manslaughter (killing someone without premeditation) ten years before. He had been sent to prison. As a part of his sentence, he had been ordered to pay restitution of $10,000 to the estate. Monthly payments were set at an amount the defendant could reasonably afford, given his income and expenses. Now the ten-year repayment period was up. The law said that his debt could be forgiven. And the court session upheld that. Yet he hadn't fulfilled his obligation because he hadn't paid off the full $10,000.

Although we don't know who was killed or who was left behind, we can assume the family of the deceased person had suffered both emotionally and financially. Was this decision justice for the family? We know that the defendant was twenty at the time he committed the crime. In addition to serving time, he made the payments that were set for him over all those ten years. Was the decision justice for the defendant?

GROUP DISCUSSION. What do you think justice means for each of the parties in the opening story?

PERSONAL REFLECTION. When have you struggled over whether justice was being done?

Justice can be a fuzzy issue for us, as it was for Israel. Time and again the prophets reminded the people that an inner attitude of righteousness is not enough. It must show in our lives; we must also be people of just action. *Read Isaiah 61.*

1. In verses 1-3 the prophet describes his call to serve. What groups are listed, and in what way do they need justice?

2. What common elements do you see among these groups?

3. What current situations do you know of that fit these categories of need?

4. How would meeting these needs for others be a sign of God's work in you (v. 3)?

5. Because Israel sinned and turned away from God, God allowed them to be conquered. How might verses 4-9 be a source of joy to them?

6. Notice the contrast in verse 8 between what the Lord loves and hates. What do this verse and verses 1-3 tell you about God's concerns?

7. In verses 10-11 the ruler describes God's work in him. What is God doing for him?

8. Compare the actions we are called to in verses 1-3 with the physical appearance of the ruler in verse 10. What is the relationship between right actions (justice) and being a righteous person?

9. Jesus applied Isaiah 61:1-2 to himself (Luke 4:16-21). How does he also fulfill the promise of verse 11?

10. What keeps you from pursuing justice?

11. How can this passage be an encouragement to you?

12. What actions can you take to bring justice to the needy?

Pray about the injustice you see around you and around the world. Ask God to teach you how he views justice.

Now or Later
Read a good book to deepen your understanding of biblical justice. One suggestion is *Good News About Injustice* by Gary Haugen (IVP).

6

Courage

In children's worship I asked the kids to tell about a time when they had experienced fear in facing a situation—when they had said "I can't do that"—and then gotten past their fear. For Bethany it was taking a big leap on the jungle gym. (She demonstrated with chairs, her dress swirling in the air.) For Amanda it was the first day of school and anxiety about whether the other kids would like her.

The times in your life when you are likely to say "No, God, I can't" may be surprisingly similar. It might be an act of physical endurance (giving birth, for example!). It might be a big job interview. Or it might be standing up to an unethical client.

GROUP DISCUSSION. Describe an "I can't" you have conquered.

PERSONAL REFLECTION. Why are you fearful in certain situations?

The courageous choice that Shadrach, Meshach and Abednego made—not to bow down to a secular idol, despite the fact that it could cost them their prestigious jobs in the king's house or even their lives—is strikingly contemporary. *Read Daniel 3.*

1. Describe the characters who play key roles in this story.

2. Who do you identify with and why?

3. What seems to be the motivation behind the actions of each character or group of characters?

4. Consider how the actions of each character or group of characters may have changed the outcome. What could have been different results depending on their responses?

5. How might Shadrach, Meshach and Abednego have rationalized bowing down to the idol?

6. When have you felt pressure to bow to the idols of the world?

7. In verses 16-18 Shadrach, Meshach and Abednego speak with theological depth. How do they describe the relationship between our will and God's?

8. What thoughts and feelings do you experience when you read of the fourth person in the furnace (v. 25)?

9. In what ways have you experienced God's comfort in times when you took a step of courage?

10. What has the king learned about God (vv. 25-30)?

11. The courage of the three Hebrew men led to greater honor in God's eyes and in the world (v. 30). Have you seen this result in the lives of Christians you know? Explain.

12. What would be an act of courage that—with God's support—you could take today?

Ask God to make you ready for risk, so that the next time he wants you to exercise courage you will do so.

Now or Later
Praying together can help us sense God's encouraging presence. Ask someone to pray with you about your need for courage.

7

Moderation

Excess is celebrated around the world. A popular U.S. fashion magazine recently had an article about the most fashion-conscious Russian women. One woman explained that the $300 she spends on one pair of shoes is what a friend earns in a month. Monthly high-fashion expenses total from $10,000 to $50,000 for this woman and others. Where the money comes from is never mentioned, but people who do business in Russia tell me that it is most certainly mafia money. It appears that the journalists were more interested in a flashy story than in the business practices of the interviewees.

Magazine articles such as this and TV shows like *MTV Cribs* or *Lifestyles of the Rich and Famous* feed the cultural myth that such irresponsible lifestyles are desirable and perhaps even attainable. By comparison, our own lifestyles most likely seem very modest, yet we feed into this myth when we follow the media hype.

GROUP DISCUSSION. Give examples of current TV shows, commercials, ad campaigns and so on that promote a lifestyle of excess.

PERSONAL REFLECTION. What excess in your own life do you
need to confess to God?

In the end, as the writer of Ecclesiastes shows, these pursuits
are meaningless. *Read Ecclesiastes 2:1-11.*

1. List the ways in which the speaker has gone about trying to
find what is good.

Which of these efforts might be seen as frivolous by popular
culture, and which might be seen as valuable endeavors?

2. What clues does the passage give as to why the speaker
might have taken on this task?

3. What are some modern-day parallels to the kinds of projects
listed in verses 4-6?

4. What ways do people try to do the types of things mentioned in verses 7-9?

---

5. In verses 3 and 9 the writer mentions that "wisdom stayed" with him.

What do you think this means?

---

6. In verse 10 he says that he delighted in his work and this was his reward, yet in verse 11 he says that his work was meaningless. What important principles about work do these two observations suggest?

---

7. What does verse 10 suggest about how we find meaning in life?

8. How does the descriptive language in verse 11 illustrate the author's point?

_____

9. What does this passage say about excess?

_____

10. How are you tempted to find meaning in excess?

_____

11. In what ways might you find a lifestyle of moderation more satisfying than a lifestyle that indulges in excess?

Pray that you will grow in your desire for the things of God.

Now or Later

Monitor your response to media this week in terms of your own desires.

8

Integrity

We hear about the scandals—the business executives who choose money, in amounts beyond imagination for most of us, over their responsibilities to employees and stockholders. In some cases their choices have brought whole companies down. But what about the ones who say no?

I have a friend who recently told me of how it had been assumed that she would join others in bending the rules at the highest level of her profession. "You scratch my back; I'll scratch yours. Everyone does it." But she didn't. And it is costly. She has not advanced to the top. She is still young—and she might. But she also knows that the choices she has made may mean that she never reaches the goal she has been working toward for years.

GROUP DISCUSSION. When do you find your ideas about integrity coming into conflict with life choices?

PERSONAL REFLECTION. When have you failed to choose the way of integrity? Begin by confessing that to God and allowing yourself to experience assurance of God's forgiveness.

In 1 Samuel 24 we meet David in a tough moment. He has been running for some time from King Saul, who is trying to kill David out of jealousy. *Read 1 Samuel 24.*

1. What strong action verbs do you notice in these verses?

2. Describe David's situation from what you know here. What would it have been like for him?

What about Saul?

3. Taking into account the relationship between David and Saul (see 1 Samuel 18 for background), how might one justify the statements David's men make in verse 4?

4. Why does David regret cutting Saul's robe (vv. 5-7)?

5. What small actions of questionable integrity are tempting for you?

6. What do you find surprising about David's actions in verses 8-15?

7. How does integrity involve risk taking?

8. How do David's words and actions show him to be a man of integrity?

9. How does Saul's response (vv. 16-22) give even more credibility to David's actions?

10. What power does integrity have to turn enemies into friends?

---

11. What current situation or relationship would you like to change through actions of integrity?

How might you do that?

Pray for understanding regarding what it means to be a person of integrity in the various situations of your life.

Now or Later
Ask God to reveal the areas of your life in which you need to grow in integrity and to give you friends who will "keep you honest."

9

Perseverance

After an accident at work, Lloyd Hotaling was told that he would never walk again. Yet in time he discovered that he could take a few steps if he leaned on two canes. Every day he would walk as far as he could, moving ever so slowly. His grandchildren recall seeing him inching along just blocks from home, and they knew it had taken him a painfully long time to get there. Yet over time his muscles were restored and he walked without any support.

Perseverance is often regarded as the quality required to reach a goal. When we work hard at something, we keep the expected reward in sight. Yet the central goal of our spiritual lives is one we will never fully achieve in this life. We must continue to move forward, growing in knowledge of Christ and becoming more like him, in confidence that the day will come when we will be made complete in heaven.

GROUP DISCUSSION. In what ways are you tempted to become complacent or discouraged about your spiritual lives?

PERSONAL REFLECTION. Who is a model for you?

In Philippians Paul offers us encouragement and inspiration to persevere in the most important part of life. *Read Philippians 3:7-16.*

1. What words and phrases in this passage characterize us as people in process?

2. In what ways do you see your own struggle to follow Christ in this text?

3. What advantages has Paul lost (see vv. 4-6)?

How does Paul's loss help him to gain Christ (vv. 7-9)?

4. How do verses 8-9 define *rubbish?*

5. What "things" in your life could be considered "rubbish"?

6. Note the things that we are to pursue in verses 10-11. How do these pursuits contrast with the rubbish in our lives?

7. What is a person who is pursuing Christ like (vv. 12, 15)?

8. Verse 13 tells us to forget what is behind and "strain toward what is ahead." Why are both aspects of this instruction important?

Which is more difficult for you? Explain.

9. What has Christ done for you that you would likely "take hold of"?

10. What does it mean to "live up to what we have already attained" (v. 16)?

11. In what area do you need encouragement to press on?

Tell God of your need for encouragement and your desire to persevere in following him. Allow yourself to receive his reassurance and love.

Now or Later

How will you persevere in your Christian life by taking steps toward growth? Set a goal.

Leader's Notes

Leading a Bible discussion can be an enjoyable and rewarding experience. But it can also be *scary*—especially if you've never done it before. If this is your feeling, you're in good company. When God asked Moses to lead the Israelites out of Egypt, he replied, "O Lord, please send someone else to do it!" (Ex 4:13). It was the same with Solomon, Jeremiah and Timothy, but God helped these people in spite of their weaknesses, and he will help you as well.

You don't need to be an expert on the Bible or a trained teacher to lead a Bible discussion. The idea behind these inductive studies is that the leader guides group members to discover for themselves what the Bible has to say. This method of learning will allow group members to remember much more of what is said than a lecture would.

These studies are designed to be led easily. As a matter of fact, the flow of questions through the passage from observation to interpretation to application is so natural that you may feel that the studies lead themselves. This study guide is also flexible. You can use it with a variety of groups—student, professional, neighborhood or church groups. Each study takes forty-five to sixty minutes in a group setting.

There are some important facts to know about group dynamics and encouraging discussion. The suggestions listed below should enable you to effectively and enjoyably fulfill your role as leader.

Preparing for the Study

1. Ask God to help you understand and apply the passage in your

own life. Unless this happens, you will not be prepared to lead others. Pray too for the various members of the group. Ask God to open your hearts to the message of his Word and motivate you to action.

2. Read the introduction to the entire guide to get an overview of the entire book and the issues which will be explored.

3. As you begin each study, read and reread the assigned Bible passage to familiarize yourself with it.

4. This study guide is based on the New International Version of the Bible. It will help you and the group if you use this translation as the basis for your study and discussion.

5. Carefully work through each question in the study. Spend time in meditation and reflection as you consider how to respond.

6. Write your thoughts and responses in the space provided in the study guide. This will help you to express your understanding of the passage clearly.

7. It might help to have a Bible dictionary handy. Use it to look up any unfamiliar words, names or places. (For additional help on how to study a passage, see chapter five of *How to Lead a LifeGuide Bible Study,* InterVarsity Press.)

8. Consider how you can apply the Scripture to your life. Remember that the group will follow your lead in responding to the studies. They will not go any deeper than you do.

9. Once you have finished your own study of the passage, familiarize yourself with the leader's notes for the study you are leading. These are designed to help you in several ways. First, they tell you the purpose the study guide author had in mind when writing the study. Take time to think through how the study questions work together to accomplish that purpose. Second, the notes provide you with additional background information or suggestions on group dynamics for various questions. This information can be useful when people have difficulty understanding or answering a question. Third, the leader's notes can alert you to potential problems you may encounter during the study.

10. If you wish to remind yourself of anything mentioned in the leader's notes, make a note to yourself below that question in the study.

Leading the Study

1. Begin the study on time. Open with prayer, asking God to help the group to understand and apply the passage.

2. Be sure that everyone in your group has a study guide. Encourage the group to prepare beforehand for each discussion by reading the introduction to the guide and by working through the questions in the study.

3. At the beginning of your first time together, explain that these studies are meant to be discussions, not lectures. Encourage the members of the group to participate. However, do not put pressure on those who may be hesitant to speak during the first few sessions. You may want to suggest the following guidelines to your group.

☐ Stick to the topic being discussed.

☐ Your responses should be based on the verses which are the focus of the discussion and not on outside authorities such as commentaries or speakers.

☐ These studies focus on a particular passage of Scripture. Only rarely should you refer to other portions of the Bible. This allows for everyone to participate in in-depth study on equal ground.

☐ Anything said in the group is considered confidential and will not be discussed outside the group unless specific permission is given to do so.

☐ We will listen attentively to each other and provide time for each person present to talk.

☐ We will pray for each other.

4. Have a group member read the introduction at the beginning of the discussion.

5. Every session begins with a group discussion question. The question or activity is meant to be used before the passage is read. The question introduces the theme of the study and encourages group members to begin to open up. Encourage as many members as possible to participate, and be ready to get the discussion going with your own response.

This section is designed to reveal where our thoughts or feelings need to be transformed by Scripture. That is why it is especially important not to read the passage before the discussion question is asked. The passage will tend to color the honest reactions people would otherwise give because they are, of course, supposed to think the way the Bible does.

You may want to supplement the group discussion question with an icebreaker to help people to get comfortable. See the community section of *Small Group Idea Book* for more ideas.

You also might want to use the personal reflection question with your group. Either allow a time of silence for people to respond individually or discuss it together.

6. Have a group member (or members if the passage is long) read aloud the passage to be studied. Then give people several minutes to read the passage again silently so that they can take it all in.

7. Question 1 will generally be an overview question designed to briefly survey the passage. Encourage the group to look at the whole passage, but try to avoid getting sidetracked by questions or issues that will be addressed later in the study.

8. As you ask the questions, keep in mind that they are designed to be used just as they are written. You may simply read them aloud. Or you may prefer to express them in your own words.

There may be times when it is appropriate to deviate from the study guide. For example, a question may have already been answered. If so, move on to the next question. Or someone may raise an important question not covered in the guide. Take time to discuss it, but try to keep the group from going off on tangents.

9. Avoid answering your own questions. If necessary, repeat or rephrase them until they are clearly understood. Or point out something you read in the leader's notes to clarify the context or meaning. An eager group quickly becomes passive and silent if they think the leader will do most of the talking.

10. Don't be afraid of silence. People may need time to think about the question before formulating their answers.

11. Don't be content with just one answer. Ask, "What do the rest of you think?" or "Anything else?" until several people have given answers to the question.

12. Acknowledge all contributions. Try to be affirming whenever possible. Never reject an answer. If it is clearly off-base, ask, "Which

verse led you to that conclusion?" or again, "What do the rest of you think?"

13. Don't expect every answer to be addressed to you, even though this will probably happen at first. As group members become more at ease, they will begin to truly interact with each other. This is one sign of healthy discussion.

14. Don't be afraid of controversy. It can be very stimulating. If you don't resolve an issue completely, don't be frustrated. Move on and keep it in mind for later. A subsequent study may solve the problem.

15. Periodically summarize what the group has said about the passage. This helps to draw together the various ideas mentioned and gives continuity to the study. But don't preach.

16. At the end of the Bible discussion you may want to allow group members a time of quiet to work on an idea under "Now or Later." Then discuss what you experienced. Or you may want to encourage group members to work on these ideas between meetings. Give an opportunity during the session for people to talk about what they are learning.

17. Conclude your time together with conversational prayer, adapting the prayer suggestion at the end of the study to your group. Ask for God's help in following through on the commitments you've made.

18. End on time.

Many more suggestions and helps are found in *How to Lead a LifeGuide Bible Study,* which is part of the LifeGuide Bible Study series.

Components of Small Groups

A healthy small group should do more than study the Bible. There are four components to consider as you structure your time together.

Nurture. Small groups help us to grow in our knowledge and love of God. Bible study is the key to making this happen and is the foundation of your small group.

Community. Small groups are a great place to develop deep friendships with other Christians. Allow time for informal interaction before and after each study. Plan activities and games that will help you get to know each other. Spend time having fun together—going on a picnic or cooking dinner together.

Worship and prayer. Your study will be enhanced by spending time praising God together in prayer or song. Pray for each other's needs—and keep track of how God is answering prayer in your group. Ask God to help you to apply what you are learning in your study.

Outreach. Reaching out to others can be a practical way of applying what you are learning, and it will keep your group from becoming self-focused. Host a series of evangelistic discussions for your friends or neighbors. Clean up the yard of an elderly friend. Serve at a soup kitchen together, or spend a day working on a Habitat house.

Many more suggestions and helps in each of these areas are found in *Small Group Idea Book.* Information on building a small group can be found in *Small Group Leaders' Handbook* and *The Big Book on Small Groups* (both from InterVarsity Press). Reading through one of these books would be worth your time.

Study 1. Faith. Ephesians 1:11-23.

Purpose: To see faith as based in the Person we believe in rather than our own strength.

Background. This book was written to encourage the churches in Asia Minor and around Ephesus to continue Paul's mission. In these verses the readers are called to remember their salvation.

Group discussion. Most of us will have some understanding and experience of both the feeling and thinking aspects of faith, but our personalities tend to push us more strongly in one direction or the other.

The opening question is designed to help the group to warm up to each other. No matter how well members of a group may know each other, there is always a stiffness that needs to be overcome before people will begin to talk openly. A good question will break the ice, get the group's attention and draw people into the discussion.

Group discussion questions can also reveal where our thoughts or feelings need to be transformed by Scripture. That is why it is especially important not to read the passage before the approach question is asked. The passage will tend to color the honest reactions people would otherwise give because they are, of course, supposed to think the way the Bible does. Giving honest responses before they find out what the Bible says may help them see where their thoughts or attitudes need to be changed.

Question 1. These verses can be seen as a brief summary of the gospel, describing what God has done for us.

Question 3. Some will read these verses as saying that we are all chosen to be with God, and others will read them as speaking of the predestination of the elect few. Here's how Andrew T. Lincoln puts it: "This clause heavily underlines that believers' appointment in Christ to their destiny is part of God's sovereign purpose . . . with the description of God as the one who carries out or works all things according to his own will" (*Ephesians* [Waco, Tex.: Word, 1990], p. 36).

Members of your group may disagree about what the implications are for all people, but Christians of either conviction can revel in the miracle of grace that has been extended.

Question 6. Sometimes immature, overzealous faith can alienate those we want to win over to Christ, especially family members. Mature faith perseveres in love even when the other person ignores or rejects the gospel. Other examples would include Muslim fundamentalists who use violence or those in cultic groups who emphasize certain practices more than faith in Christ.

Question 7. Andrew Lincoln offers the following insight: "In the O.T., wisdom often involves practical knowledge, the ability to choose right conduct, while in Paul it often involves understanding God's activity in Christ and the benefits it brings to believers" (*Ephesians*, pp. 56-57).

Questions 8-9. Some Christian groups tend to emphasize faith and others experience, but verses 17-20 show how the two are intertwined. Knowledge brings a deep inner experience of faith. Experience in turn supports and bolsters our faith.

Question 11. This passage draws us to see that our faith is true because of who Christ is and not because of how strongly we believe. These verses call us away from self-sufficient behavior, such as trying harder to believe certain truths, studying more or praying more, that takes the focus off Christ.

Between studies. To help integrate the virtues as you go along, encourage group members to consider the following questions each week between meetings: (1) Which virtue have you had an opportunity to exercise this week? (2) Which virtue has been a struggle for you and why? Then follow up at the beginning or end of each study and discuss your progress in making these virtues a part of your lives.

Study 2. Hope. Psalm 71.

Purpose: To show how hopelessness results from focusing inward, while keeping our focus on the God who restores hope.

Question 1. *The NIV Study Bible* points out the confident expression of hope at the center of the passage (vv. 14-16) "framed by an appeal for help" (vv. 1-4) and a vow to praise in anticipation of deliverance (vv. 22-24). The second and fifth stanzas have references to times of trouble (v. 7: "like a portent" and v. 20). Stanzas three and four point out that the king is aging.

Question 2. David seems to move back and forth between declaring his hope in the Lord and presenting his plea for help (see, for example, v. 1 and vv. 8-9). It seems that by recalling how God has been faithful to him in the past (v. 17) David is reminding himself that he can be confident about his future (vv. 20-21).

Question 5. Because this psalm was evidently written late in life, David has the luxury of looking back to see what God has done for him over the years. Verses 5 and 6 show that David recognizes God's hand guiding him throughout his life. Verse 7 refers to David as a "portent." This could mean either that (1) David was seen as a shining example of God's care or that (2) David was seen as one who had received God's judgment. Either would make sense in David's life, but in each case David recognizes that it is God who has protected him even when he did not deserve it (Marvin E. Tate, *Psalms 51-100* [Waco, Tex.: Word, 1990], p. 214).

Question 6. A couple of factors likely come into play here: David is aging and seems to fear the weakness that comes with old age (vv. 9, 18), and David still has enemies who pursue him (vv. 4, 10, 24).

Question 8. In verses 14-24 David praises God for his loving actions in the past and also for what David expects God to do in the future.

Question 9. In the process of offering his praise to God, David recalls how good God is, and that gives him greater confidence about his own future.

Question 10. If time allows, you can discuss how God is currently encouraging you, or you can make this the subject of closing prayer.

Study 3. Love. 1 John 3:11-20.

Purpose: To see how love grows out of putting our faith and hope in Christ.

Group discussion. Help the group to think of a variety of relationships that require some type of love to be healthy. Friendships and family, for example, are important areas of life that need love as much as the sexual/romantic love usually featured in the media.

Question 4. Cain's story is told in Genesis 4:1-12.

Question 5. The thought in verse 13 echoes the words of Jesus in John 15:18-19. This verse is connected to verse 12, where Cain's actions were explained as resulting from a realization that Abel's actions were more righteous. When Christians show their love, the world is forced to recognize its own unrighteousness. Note also that verse 13 is sometimes translated "that the world hates you" (NRSV) or "when the world hates you" (The Message), implying that when Christians love as Jesus has commanded, the world will respond negatively.

Question 7. Though we may not literally be called to lay down our lives, we can give up our own interests for the sake of others in many small ways at work and at home. A more direct parallel comes from the lives of the parents of an eight-year-old child who died. In the midst of their grief and the need to make decisions about burial and so on, they made the choice to give the liver of their son to a ten-month-old baby in need of a transplant. Both families are Christian.

Another example of sacrifice comes from college chaplain Tim Dearborn. Injured in a boating accident in Alaska, Dearborn needed blood transfusions. Because there was no blood bank in the town, an appeal for donors went out on the radio.

"Weeks after my discharge from the hospital . . . I was taking my first walk down the main street of the town. Life seemed so full and good. The air smelled purer; the sea gulls and even the ravens sounded more melodious. . . . The pharmacist emerged from his store. I'd never met him before, but he called me by name. He asked me how I was feeling and then said, 'Praise God that you've recovered. You better take good care of yourself. I've a pint of my blood invested in you.'

"My very life had become for him an icon. His blood given for me—a physical reminder of Christ's blood given for us" (*Taste & See* [Downers Grove, Ill.: InterVarsity Press, 1996], p. 82).

Question 9. In the presence of a holy God we become aware of the sin in our hearts. Verses 19-20 seem to assume that we will have a certain "guilty conscience" when we are before God. However, reassurance is offered that if we love "with actions and in truth," then we can be sure that God will accept us, regardless of how unworthy we feel. Verse 19 may be translated with the future tense "we shall know," according to one translator, and perhaps suggests a crisis in which we will need reassurance, rather than implying a constant certainty that we are "on God's side." So this may be referring to a final sort of judgment or to God's ongoing judgment. In verse 20, while divine judgment is not excluded, John's main purpose is to "reassure his readers that when believers are most aware of their shortcomings in respect of God's standards, the love and mercy of the Father are present to heal their troubled consciences" (Stephen S. Smalley, *1, 2, 3 John* [Waco, Tex.: Word, 1984], p. 203).

Questions 10-11. As these questions are discussed, the leader needs to model vulnerability by responding to them with specific honest comments.

Study 4. Wisdom. 1 Corinthians 1:18-31.

Purpose: To look at wisdom in light of the cross rather than in light of the world.

Question 1. Help the group begin to recognize the different meanings Paul gives to wisdom and foolishness in this passage. Paul is using a form of irony in this passage; group members may miss it if they aren't looking for it. It may be helpful to insert "so-called" before the references to wisdom and wise people in verse 20. Also, note that verse 19 is a reference to Isaiah 29:14, where God promises to turn the religious expectations of Israel upside down.

Question 3. Be sure that the group picks up on God's role in helping us to see the wisdom of the cross—and that they also recognize the role of faith in understanding the cross.

Question 5. Again, note Paul's tone in the passage. Also, discuss the ways in which God's view turns everything upside down and completely alters our understanding of the world.

Question 6. This question is not intended to begin a lengthy debate about the relative merits of secular learning. Rather, it is intended to help us think about how we may sometimes leave God in the church while we go about our weekday lives with the same worldview as the secular world. This may mean we are putting our faith in things considered wise by the world but not considered so by God.

Question 10. This verse refers to Jeremiah 9:23-24, another passage about how the wise, strong and rich need to boast about their understanding of God instead of about their wisdom, strength or wealth. For those who are fascinated with the idea of boasting, see also 2 Corinthians 11, where Paul does a little boasting of his own.

Study 5. Justice. Isaiah 61.

Purpose: To learn about how the Lord regards justice and how we can become people who practice justice.

Group discussion. Don't allow this question to derail your group into a lengthy political and social debate. An alternate opening question would be "Who in your community needs justice?"

Question 1. There are many similar passages in which the prophets call the people to justice and describe how God blesses just actions. See, for example, Micah 3.

Jesus quoted verses 1 and 2 in reference to himself (Lk 4:16-21). According to *The NIV Study Bible*, verse 1 "may refer to Isaiah in a limited sense, but the Messianic servant is the main figure intended" (Kenneth Barker, ed. [Grand Rapids, Mich.: Zondervan, 1985], p. 1106).

The events in these verses are comparable to those in the Year of Jubilee (Lev 25) when debts were to be forgiven, slaves released and land returned to its original owners.

Question 2. These are voiceless people (children, women, prisoners) and the oppressed (slaves, the poor).

Question 3. Consider groups of people and personal acquaintances such as abuse victims, those in poverty, prisoners and victims of war.

Question 4. According to John D. W. Watts, "The chapter contains a balanced picture of ministries for God's peoples. The spirit-anointed preacher of good news to the disadvantaged and oppressed continues the role of the suffering one of 50:4-9 and 52:13—53:12. He is God's direct line of communication to the outsiders, the needy and distressed" (*Isaiah 34—66* [Waco, Tex.: Word, 1987], p. 305). In Luke's Gospel, Jesus emphasizes that he has come for all people, not just the rich and powerful. These are the people to whom God wants us to demonstrate his love.

Question 5. In verses 4-7 and 10-11, Watts suggests that we have a new speaker, an administrator or ruler. The speaker may be Artaxerxes (Ezra 7:12-29). These verses would refer to "his success in stabilizing his regime and in winning full control of Palestine" (*Isaiah 34—66*, p. 304). Others feel that it is the prophet or "Anointed One" whose voice continues throughout this passage (see J. Alec Motyer, *The Prophecy of Isaiah* [Downers Grove, Ill.: InterVarsity Press, 1993], pp. 499-505). Note also that in verses 8-9 the speaker is Yahweh.

Question 6. Throughout Scripture we see God's concern for voiceless people. For example, in Deuteronomy 10:18 we are told to defend orphans and widows and give help to aliens. Psalm 10 reminds us to care for the helpless (v. 12) and mentions "the fatherless and the oppressed" (vv. 17-18). Jesus refers to the Isaiah passage in Luke 4:17-19 as well.

Question 12. If none of you know of any outlets for service, this question will be frustrating for your group. Come with some ideas you could do together—helping out at a Habitat for Humanity building site, serving at a soup kitchen, sorting out baby clothes at a crisis pregnancy center. It doesn't have to be a huge project. Just plan to do something.

Study 6. Courage. Daniel 3.

Purpose: To provide encouragement for Christians to maintain their unique identity even in a hostile environment.

Questions 1-4. List details about Nebuchadnezzar, the astrologers, and Shadrach, Meshach and Abednego. More background on Shadrach, Meshach and Abednego and their relationship with Nebuchadnezzar can be found in Daniel 1—2. They would have been part of the group of officials mentioned in verse 3 because the king had made them advisors (2:49).

Question 4. It is encouraging to note that the ungodly actions on the part of Nebuchadnezzar and the astrologers led to God's being glorified by Shadrach, Meshach and Abednego.

Question 5. One way of looking at it might be to say that they should make use of their place of power and influence: perhaps if they would bow down now, they could later develop a stronger relationship with the king and gradually influence him to see their way. This is the sort of approach we take when we assume we can shape our own futures better than God can.

Question 6. Depending on the group's response, a possible follow-up question would be "When is it tempting for you to bypass one of God's commands?"

Question 7. They fully believe that God can rescue them (v. 17), yet they acknowledge that he may not do so (v. 18). They tell the king that either way they will follow God's commands.

Question 8. Psalm 91:9-16 promises that God commands his angels to guard those who love him and "acknowledge" his name. According to the *New Bible Commentary:* "Early Christian commentators viewed the fourth figure as an appearance of the Son of God or as the angel of the Lord (see v. 28) and have been frequently followed. The emphasis, however, is on the completeness of God's protection shown by the fact that they emerged without even the *smell of fire on them* (27)" (G. J. Wenham, ed., *New Bible Commentary,* 21st Century Edition [Downers Grove, Ill.: InterVarsity Press, 1994], p. 752). We can take this verse as an example of how God offers us comfort and encouragement through the hard times.

Question 10. The king moves from referring to the fourth person as "a son of the gods" (v. 25)—a pagan reference—to calling the man "an angel" (v. 28). He refers to their God as "the Most High God" (v. 26). He knows that "no other god can save." And he realizes that those who trust in God can be trusted by him (v. 30).

Question 11. Many may feel that worldly honor for being faithful to God is not a typical experience for Christians today. Yet perhaps you can think of examples in your community in which people who are honest in business and professional work are well thought of. It takes great courage to stand apart from accepted gray areas where corners are cut and morals are questionable. Many Christians on university campuses and in other settings are pressured to uphold "tolerance" as the highest value while New Age practices and other religions are embraced.

Study 7. Moderation. Ecclesiastes 2:1-11.

Purpose: To expose cultural myths about excess as a source of meaning in life and to discover how to find satisfaction in moderation.

Group discussion. You might also encourage the group to explore the implicit values and meaning that are communicated along with the "worldly" lifestyle. Also encourage people to think of not just the most outrageous examples but of some that affect them. If you prefer, you might simply ask, "Where have you observed excesses in lifestyle?"

Background. The author of Ecclesiastes is never named in the text. Many people have noted that the experiences related in the book sound very much like what we know of King Solomon. This is especially true in the passage used for this study. However, it could have been a later writer with similar experiences or even someone writing from Solomon's perspective.

It is also interesting to note that Ecclesiastes names God only once. This is a very secular struggle on the part of the writer, yet we know that God is in the background of his life.

Question 1. Be sure that the group notes both the types of endeavors made by the speaker and the scope of those endeavors. For example, he not only owned livestock, he had "more herds and flocks than anyone in Jerusalem before me."

Question 2. The book of Ecclesiastes is itself primarily hindsight commentary and analysis from one who has struggled to find meaning and true profit from what life has to offer. These verses reveal part of that struggle and search as the author tries to find meaning and value in pleasure. It is important to remember that the various activities were pursued not for their own sake but so that the author could find some ultimate meaning. In many ways, then, the author of Ecclesiastes can be seen as someone who is very contemporary. Many people today look to various activities to give their lives meaning.

Question 6. These questions may lead you into a discussion about the meaning of work. Compare the biblical statements to some common assumptions we make today about work. For example, when people ask "What do you do?" they usually expect to hear what your paid job is. Or talk about the ways in which we categorize people whose job status is less than we think it should be.

Question 10. Consider not just the areas of life in which you are tempted to excess but also what sorts of activities and events lead you into that temptation.

Question 11. It may be helpful to talk in the group about what a lifestyle of excess looks like. There are at least two ways to think of excess. One is to simply look at how much we have or do in a certain area of life. Another is to look at the contrast between what we have and do and what is actually necessary. A lifestyle of moderation can likewise be seen as how little we have and do. Or we can look at how closely what we have and do matches what we actually need.

Study 8. Integrity. 1 Samuel 24.

Purpose: To discover how our character and our relationships are affected when we are people of integrity.

Group discussion. You might get at this question by focusing on various subgroups in people's lives—extended family, church, work.

Question 1. There are powerful verbs throughout this passage, such as *crept, cut off, rebuked, attack, bowed, prostrated, delivered, urged, kill, spared, understand, recognize, hunting, avenge.*

Question 3. Saul had become jealous of David. 1 Samuel 18:12 tells us: "Saul was afraid of David, because the LORD was with David but had left Saul." Further David was successful in everything he did (18:13). Thus Saul saw that David would have continued success, power and popularity because God was with him. (See G. J. Wenham, *New Bible Commentary,* p. 314.) In 1 Samuel 18:28-29 we read that Saul became David's enemy, and he ordered his men to kill David (19:1). David and his men (1 Sam 23:13 says there were 600 men, though we don't know exactly how many were in the cave) were hiding from Saul.

Question 4. We see in the text David's great respect for "the LORD's anointed." This is further emphasized by 1 Samuel 26:9-11, a similar account. According to the Word Biblical Commentary *1 Samuel* (Ralph W. Klein [Waco, Tex.: Word, 1983], p. 239), David's cutting of Saul's robe echoes 15:27, in which Saul tore Samuel's robe. It could be read as a sign that the kingdom would be torn from Saul (see, for example, 1 Kings 11:29-31). If so, then that would explain David's reaction. Possession of even part of the royal robe might imply that David was "the legitimate heir" (see 18:4). Later in the passage (v. 12), David shows the piece as a sign of his innocence, bypassing a chance to take Saul's life.

Question 7. In the text David takes a big risk by showing himself to Saul and acknowledging what he has done. Move from the biblical example to how this connects to life today.

Study 9. Perseverance. Philippians 3:7-16.

Purpose : To inspire us to continue on in knowing Christ, looking toward the day when we will be in heaven with him.

Question 3. The verses just prior to this passage contain a list of the various advantages that Paul had either inherited or achieved in his life before he encountered Jesus on the road to Damascus (Acts 9). As a Jew attempting to merit God's favor, Paul's accomplishments were considerable. However, those achievements were themselves keeping him from seeing his need for salvation through Jesus. He could not continue to put his faith in his own accomplishments and also put his faith in Jesus.

Question 4. Paul's use of *rubbish* should be seen not only as a comparison between what we have without Jesus and what Jesus offers us. It is also a condemnation of those things that give us false hope in ourselves and make us act as if we don't really need God's gifts.

Question 5. Help the group keep in mind that this entire section is very autobiographical. Paul is speaking of the things in his life that kept him from Jesus. Those very things could have been helpful to someone else. It would be a mistake to think that each person would struggle with the same issues. For example, some people find that theological education helps them to know and understand God better, while for others it only increases their tendencies toward self-sufficiency. The important issue is for each person to be able to identify what keeps him or her from being dependent on God's grace alone.

Question 6. When we are pursuing Christ, many things that used to seem important and absorbed much of our time and energy—reaching a goal at work, getting the house in order, buying a new car before the old one falls apart—pale in comparison. This does not mean that we should be careless about our earthly responsibilities but that we should always measure our lives by our growth in knowing Christ.

Some group members may wonder at Paul's choice of words about the resurrection in verse 11. For Paul, "the resurrection is certain; the intervening events are uncertain," according to J. A. Motyer (*The Message of Philippians* [Downers Grove, Ill.: InterVarsity Press, 1984], p. 170).

Question 8. There are two dangers in remembering what is behind: we may become complacent or we may become discouraged. In this passage Paul is probably addressing those who think they have reached a spiritual level which no longer requires that they "press on." At the same time, some people look back on the mistakes they have made and see no hope that they can persevere long enough to reach the goal.

Question 10. In this verse Paul reminds us that gifts from God to us require an active response from us. Perhaps Paul meant it as a paraphrase of Jesus' words in Luke 12:47-48.

Cindy Bunch is a senior editor for InterVarsity Press. She is also the author of the LifeGuide® Bible Study Woman of God *and coauthor of* How to Lead a LifeGuide Bible Study.

What Should We Study Next?

A good place to continue your study of Scripture would be with a book study. Many groups begin with a Gospel such as *Mark* (20 studies by Jim Hoover) or *John* (26 studies by Douglas Connelly). These guides are divided into two parts so that if twenty or twenty-six weeks seems like too much to do at once, the group can feel free to do half and take a break with another topic. Later you might want to come back to it. You might prefer to try a shorter letter. *Philippians* (9 studies by Donald Baker), *Ephesians* (11 studies by Andrew T. and Phyllis J. Le Peau) and *1 & 2 Timothy and Titus* (11 studies by Pete Sommer) are good options. If you want to vary your reading with an Old Testament book, consider *Ecclesiastes* (12 studies by Bill and Teresa Syrios) for a challenging and exciting study.

There are a number of interesting topical LifeGuide studies as well. Here are some options for filling three or four quarters of a year:

Basic Discipleship
Christian Beliefs, 12 studies by Stephen D. Eyre
Christian Character, 12 studies by Andrea Sterk & Peter Scazzero
Christian Disciplines, 12 studies by Andrea Sterk & Peter Scazzero
Evangelism, 12 studies by Rebecca Pippert & Ruth Siemens

Building Community
Fruit of the Spirit, 9 studies by Hazel Offner
Spiritual Gifts, 12 studies by Charles & Anne Hummel
Christian Community, 10 studies by Rob Suggs

Character Studies
David, 12 studies by Jack Kuhatschek
New Testament Characters, 12 studies by Carolyn Nystrom
Old Testament Characters, 12 studies by Peter Scazzero
Women of the Old Testament, 12 studies by Gladys Hunt

The Trinity
Meeting God, 12 studies by J. I. Packer
Meeting Jesus, 13 studies by Leighton Ford
Meeting the Spirit, 10 studies by Douglas Connelly